The Benefits They Receive When Kids Work

By Craig A. Anderson

Overflowing Resources Publishing Company
2620 S. Cleveland, Suite 205
St. Joseph, MI 49085

ISBN: 978-1-950012-02-2

United States of America

Overflowing Resources Publishing Company is a division of Family Focused Financial. www.famfocfinancial.com

Securities and Advisory Services offered through ***Harbour Investments, Inc.*** Member SIPC.

The examples in this book are for illustrative purposes and are not intended to provide individual financial, tax, or legal advice. Every family situation is unique. Please consult a professional regarding your specific situation.

Cover design by Advisors Excel Creative and Jenny Cummings.

Kids Work / Craig A. Anderson—1st ed.

Table of Contents

Introduction

As a financial advisor for over twenty years, I have met hundreds of families. A noticeable trend over the last several years is an increasing number of families having children in their early twenties to late thirties still living with them. Often, this is a temporary situation between college and work. But many times, these kids haven't found themselves, let alone a job. It leaves the parents and their kids in limbo.

In the developed world we no longer experience grinding poverty as at the beginning of the industrial revolution. Our workplaces are much safer now, and most children are not required to work to survive. But, in many cases the pendulum has swung all the way to the other end of the spectrum, where children are being deprived in a different way. Many do not have access to one of the most rewarding opportunities of the growing-up process—work. The purpose of this story is not to suggest we should return to the abuses of the industrial revolution, but to push the pendulum back toward a more balanced position. What I want to convey through this story is how many benefits come from working. The sooner kids learn this, the sooner they can reap these benefits and be prepared for adulthood.

This book is not about teaching kids to do chores around the house. There are many good books written on that subject. After reading this story, opening one of those books might be a great next step, but this story is for the parents who are not sure what they think about their kids working—especially outside the home. I hope you will enjoy the story and reach some personal clarity along the way.

Credits

No matter how many people read through a transcript, each succeeding one seems to notice certain improvements that make it even better. So, the temptation is to review indefinitely. However, at some point we need to stop trying to perfect a work and get it out the door.

Thank you to the following people I deeply respect, whose input helped make each manuscript of this book even better.

Jody Anderson
Jenny Cummings
Linda Diltz
Tiffany Strother-Good
Janis Guckenberger
Peggy Judge
Jeff Miller
David & Wanda Shock
Vanessa Williams
Tammie Zebell

Chapter 1

Shawn glanced over his shoulder. Seeing no one, he hurried up beside James who was walking to school.

Shawn: Hey, James. T's been askin' about you. You should come by tonight, or I think he'll come lookin' for you.

James: Yeah, I've been pretty busy. The judge's got me meetin' with an old dude since I was gonna go to jail if I didn't.

Shawn: I get that. But, bro, I don't think you want to get on T's bad side. Plus, me an' the guys think you've been actin' kinda different.

James: Nah, it's me.

Shawn: No, somethin's different. You think you're better than us?

James: No.

Shawn: Then come with us Saturday. We're gonna hit that old gas station on Main. T says the cameras are out.

James: I've got stuff to do. I don't think I can go.

Shawn: This is what I'm talkin' about, J.

James: Look, Shawn, I don't wanna' go to jail. I'm just sortin' things out. Okay?

Shawn: Too good for us.

James: I just don't see it that way.

Shawn: You know what? I gotta go. I'll be seein' you, James. Have fun bein' a good boy.

Shawn was his oldest friend, and James wished he could make him understand his tight spot.

Later that same day James was walking home from school, and a car pulled up and stopped next to him. James could tell out of the corner of his eye who it was.

T: Hey, young blood, I ain't seen you around. Why don't you get in?

James: I'm good.

T: I'm not gonna ask you twice.

He heard a click and saw a gun pointing out the window at him. James was trying to stay calm, but he was afraid T could hear his heart pounding. He could hardly think.

T: You know what this means, young blood?

James was frozen in time. Should he run? He'd known T long enough to know this might not be a bluff. Would he die today? Should he get in the car? What would his mother say if he went back to the gang? What would Mr. Powers say? Why did he care what Mr. Powers would say? He felt fear and anger rising.

Chapter 2

Five weeks earlier

It was Saturday morning. Ron Power's wife, Jackie, was at the farmer's market. Ron was supposed to be showing houses to a young couple, but one of them was sick, so they cancelled. This gave Ron a chance to wash and wax his Ford Mustang Boss 351. On the outside it was a plain looking sedan. But under the hood it was *all go, no show!* As a young boy, he had ambitions to race professionally. Now he was happy to watch NASCAR races on TV and spend some of his free time repairing, tweaking, cleaning, and shining his hobby car.

Just then he felt a presence. Ron glanced up and saw that it was Olivia Davis, his next-door neighbor. He didn't know her very well, although she had lived there with her boys for a year now, maybe two. Jackie had invited them over to eat several times, but Olivia was very busy raising two sons and working two jobs. As he straightened up, he noticed tears in her eyes. Ron was the type of person who, when he saw anyone in distress, was immediately and completely there to help.

Ron: Olivia, what's wrong?

Olivia: Ron, I'm sorry. I just don't know who else to talk to.

Ron, *inviting*: Tell me what's going on.

Something in Ron's compassionate demeanor made her slightly more comfortable.

Olivia, *pausing to collect herself:* Ron, James is in trouble. *Her anxiety was obvious.*

Ron: Is he your oldest?

Olivia: Yes, he's fifteen, almost sixteen.

Ron: What's happening?

Olivia bit her lip in hesitation, then made up her mind.

Olivia: Ron, I don't want you to think badly of James, but … well … he was caught robbing a convenience store.

Olivia could not even look at Ron while she spoke. Ron could see that she was ashamed for her family, and her son.

Ron: Olivia, sometimes kids do dumb things.

He didn't want to minimize the seriousness of the situation but wanted to reassure her that he didn't think badly of them.

Olivia: They have it all on video, but that's not the worst part. He's part of a gang, and this is not the first time he's been involved in something like this.

Ron: Oh.

Olivia, *looking up at Ron for the first time in the conversation:* Ron, I grew up in a rough neighborhood just three miles from here. I went to Jefferson.

Ron knew the school. When he played football against Jefferson growing up, school administrators and police would try to ensure fights did not turn into riots. Today a much larger police presence tried to prevent small wars from breaking out between schools and gangs.

Ron: I do think you mentioned that when we met. Not the safest school.

Olivia: Well, school was safe compared to being home with my parents. They were on again, off again. My dad was not around very often, but when he was, the house was a ticking time bomb. You never knew when it was going to go off, but it was *always* going to go off. I think I excelled at school so I could stay there … and hide.

My teachers, two of them, believed in me. They filled me full of hopes and dreams, said education was the key to a good job, and a good job was the key to getting out of the bad part of town and all the junk going on there. I dearly loved the attention and affirmation I was getting from them. Lord knows, I wasn't getting that kind of treatment at home. I studied hard, got scholarships, and was the first in my family to go to college.

Ron: I never knew all that. Good for you. *Then he reflected.* And you're a nurse now?

Olivia: *A voice in her head made Olivia wonder why she was sharing so many of the details of her life, but she felt so comfortable and safe talking to this man.* Yes. Between my nursing job, and my weekend job, I make enough money to support us and live here.

Ron: You work very hard.

Olivia: I do, and I'm glad to, but my teachers were wrong. I mean, we didn't escape anything. I should've seen this coming. I didn't want to believe this could happen. I felt so proud, like such a good mother for getting my kids out of there. But that environment followed me here.

Ron: What do you mean by that?

Ron thought he knew, but he also knew that Olivia needed to talk this through.

Olivia: You can find bad people wherever you go.

Ron: That's true.

Olivia: That's what James did. He found bad kids to hang out with. I wanted to think they were just friends watching movies or playing video games together, but I think they've been out on the streets and stealing for a while now.

The funny thing is … I thought I had left all the bad stuff in my old neighborhood, but he never got into trouble until we moved here.

She sighed.

I feel like I have failed as a parent. I have no idea what to do. I love my boys so much I've never held back anything to give them a better life. My heart could burst when I think about how much I love my kids!

With that, Olivia did burst into tears. Ron was feeling awkward and wondering what he could do. Just then, Jackie came home from the farmer's market. She got out to greet Olivia and saw the tears. She instinctively moved to her and wrapped her arms around her. Olivia melted into the slightly older woman.

Olivia: I'm so sorry to be doing this, *she sobbed.* I promise I didn't mean to come over here and make a mess of myself.

Jackie: Don't you worry about it. Can we go inside?

Olivia looked miserable and grateful. As they came inside, Ron offered Olivia a seat on the couch and Jackie poured her a mug of coffee.

Jackie: I don't know what's going on, but I can see you're having a tough time. If you feel like it, can you catch me up?

They did, and once Olivia had completely gotten ahold of herself, she was able to get to the real point of her visit.

Olivia: I have a big favor to ask of you, Mr. Powers.

Ron: Please, call me Ron.

Olivia: Ron, we hardly know each other. *Tears threatened to start again, but Olivia regained composure.* But I can just tell what kind of people you are, and … well … I wanted to know if you could help me with this.

Ron: Olivia, you're right, we don't know you and your family very well, but I can assure you, we care about you, and we're glad that you're a neighbor. I'll help if I can.

Olivia knew that he meant it. One look into the man's eyes told of his sincerity. Although she had learned by experience not to trust certain men, she instinctively, but cautiously, trusted Ron Powers.

Olivia: I went down to the courthouse to see what I could find out before James goes to see the judge. I got to talking with a nice lady there who told me that she couldn't give me any *advice*, but she kind of did. She said kids who go into a juvenile center just get worse, and usually end up in prison. I already knew that. Then she asked if I knew anybody who would be willing to mentor James, because if I did, the judge might allow that instead of him going to juvie, since he is a minor and this is his first offense. There is no one in my family or old neighborhood that … well, there just isn't anyone … but I thought maybe you would be willing to ….

Ron: I see.

Olivia knew this was an imposition. She tried with all her might to avoid crying again because she did not want to manipulate Ron into taking this on. She knew it would be hard and it might fail. Jackie, perceptive as ever, moved to hug her again. Jackie was crying too. The show of kindness brought another stream of tears to Olivia's face. The women mourned together as Ron considered her request.

Jackie looked at Ron as they held a brief, but silent conversation. There was no question she wanted him to do what Olivia was asking. Still, Ron was not naive enough to think he could just swoop in and fix everything.

Ron, *breaking the silence:* Olivia, I would need to know what this looks like, but of course I'll do what I can.

Olivia: I don't know exactly what it entails. I didn't even want to suggest it to the judge unless I knew I had someone I could trust who could step in and help. *She looked down reflectively*, I have worked so hard for these boys. I can't believe it's come to this.

Jackie: You have done an amazing job, Olivia. Anyone can see that.

Olivia: Even though we don't know each other that well, I've noticed when your kids stop by your house, they seem well adjusted. And Jerry seems very nice. I thought you must be doing something right with them.

Ron, *laughing*: We can assure you that we've made lots of mistakes and our kids are not perfect. But they are good kids, and we are blessed to have them. If we have any wisdom, we're happy to share it.

Jackie: No matter what happens now, I'm glad you came over. We feel honored that you would trust us.

Olivia: I don't want to see my kids end up like so many others where I grew up. That's not why I work so hard. I want them to make it so they can be a positive influence in the world. I had such dreams for them when they were born.

Ron: Don't give up on those dreams yet, Olivia. And I'm happy to speak with the judge if he agrees to that. Just let me know.

Olivia: Thank you, both of you, so much.

Chapter 3

Three weeks later

Olivia was sitting at Ron and Jackie's kitchen table with them. Ron gave her an overview of his plan.

Olivia: Ron, I am so grateful you met with the judge, and you're taking this seriously. But I must be honest, you put a lot of emphasis on him working. You say in your plan that you would like to pay James to help you around the yard, and then you would like to help him get a regular job.

Jackie: Is there something wrong with that?

Olivia: I'm not comfortable with James getting a job so young. I like the part about him helping you around your house, but I don't want you to pay him.

Ron: Why is that?

Olivia: My childhood wasn't safe or fun. I want my boys to have a childhood. Not only that, but it's also my job to provide for them as their mother. I want them to do well in school, without a lot of other responsibilities.

Ron: You are very responsible, Olivia.

Olivia: I try to be.

Ron: Isn't that exactly what James needs to learn—responsibility?

Olivia, *after pausing to think:* Well, that's part of why I want to be a good example to the boys. So, when they grow up, they will be responsible.

Ron: That makes sense. Can I ask you a question? Why do you work so hard?

Olivia, *pausing again:* In my neighborhood, a lot of folks were on welfare and a lot of them were on drugs. Two different chains—both prisons that hold you captive. I wanted my kids to be free. School was my ticket to work, and work was my ticket to escape that way of life for me and my boys.

Ron: So, you don't want them to do drugs or be on welfare?

Olivia: Right. And I want them to focus on school, like I did.

Ron: Michael seems very bright.

Olivia: Oh yes! He loves school like I did.

Ron: What if school is never going to be James' thing?

Olivia, *after a long stare at Ron and a big sigh of disappointment*: I'm afraid of that.

Jackie: Afraid of what?

Olivia: I've been pushing James to get good grades so he can go to college.

Jackie: Olivia, there are a lot of jobs he could excel at without going to college.

Olivia: Like what?

Ron: He could be a mechanic, plumber, welder, or an electrician. He could build things or install things or fix things or own a business.

Olivia: Okay, I can see that. But I'm still not comfortable with him working a regular job while he's in school.

Ron: Are you afraid it will get in the way of his studies?

Olivia: Yeah.

Ron: There is something else to consider ….

Olivia: Uh huh?

Ron, *smiling:* It might get in the way of some other things, too.

Olivia, *her smile saying, "good point"*: I'll think about it.

Chapter 4

The next day

Ron and James were sitting at Ron's kitchen table.

Ron: Why don't you start by telling me what happened?

James was quiet and trying to play tough. At fifteen he was starting to fill out and already looked formidable. Ron wondered if it would be a good idea, along with work, for James to get into a sport at school.

Ron: James, I'm happy to work with you, but you need to work with me.

James is still quiet, looking out the window.

Ron, *pausing another 30 seconds*: All right. It's okay, James. *Ron is speaking gently.* We don't need to do this if you aren't willing. But I made a commitment to the judge, so now we go back and tell him you'd rather go to juvie.

James, *glaring at Ron angrily:* Okay! What do ya' want me t' say?

Ron: Tell me what happened.

James: You know what happened, man.

Ron: I know what others have said. I've seen the police report, but I want to hear your side.

James: It don't really matter.

Ron: It matters to me.

James: Okay, fine. We rolled up to this place. I went in and took what I wanted, along with money from the register. Cameras got it all.

Ron: Was this the first time?

James thought for a minute.

James: No. But it was the first time we hit *that* store.

Ron: Okay. Can you tell me about the first time you robbed any store?

James: I've been doing this for almost a year, man. We started with little stuff. Just lift it and put it in our pockets, ya' know?

Ron just kept listening.

James: I was real good with my hands. Then we started usin' guns and goin' for cash.

Ron: And you were never caught before?

James: I was caught once by a guy workin', and he called the cops.

Ron: But you didn't stop stealing?

James, *smiling*: Nah, the cops came and asked him a bunch of questions, but nothin' really happened. We went and robbed another place the next day.

Ron: You seem proud of yourself.

James: It ain't really like that.

Ron: Oh?

James: It ain't about pride, it's about gettin' what's yours.

Ron: But it's not yours.

James: It's all mine if I take it. That's how it is, baby.

Ron looked at James for a minute.

James: What're ya' lookin' at?

Ron: I don't know, James. I find it hard to believe that that's how your mother raised you.

James: It ain't. But that's how the streets raised me.

Ron: You have a bed, food on the table, and a mother who would do anything for you. You don't live on the streets, James. You have a family.

James looked down.

Ron: How did you get started?

James: Like I said, it was maybe a year ago. Mom was pushin' me real hard, but I was failin' at school, 'cuz, ya' know, who cares about that stuff?

Me and my friend were walkin' to the park to play ball when this sweet car rolled up. My friend was like, "Yo man, how do I get a ride like that?" This man said, "If you really want to know, get in." And that's how it started. Jus' like that.

Ron: Do you still know that man?

James, *chuckling*: Yeah, you could say that.

Ron: Is he the reason you steal?

James: You could say that, too.

Ron: Why?

James: That's how it is. If I'm gonna come up, I gotta start small.

Ron: Then what?

James: Then the sky's the limit. I'm makin' a name for myself. That's what matters.

Ron: Why?

James: 'Cuz if you ain't somebody, you ain't nobody.

Ron thought for a moment.

Ron: James, I don't buy it. I admit that I don't know you very well. We've only talked a couple times since you lived here, but I'm getting to know your mom, and I don't think this is the real James.

James: You're crazy.

Ron: I don't think so. I guess you have a choice to make. You can go to juvie, or you can come work for me.

James: Oh, I see how it is. Ya' got free help now.

Ron: This is a paid job. You are a smart young man, responsible for your own decisions. And you have a *big* decision to make right now.

He stared at James for what seemed like five minutes. Then he turned and walked upstairs.

James realized this was not someone to mess with. Ron was usually so mild mannered, but there was something in his eyes. He didn't know what it was, but he'd rather not ever again be on the receiving end of that look. There was no malice, just pure power. James wondered how he did that.

He quietly slipped out the door and went home. A few minutes later there was a knock at the door. When Ron came to answer it, James was standing there, looking down.

James: What do I gotta do?

Ron: Let's start here. Come back tomorrow and start working for me. I'll pay you minimum wage until we see what kind of worker you are. And when you're with me you're going to speak properly, the way your mother taught you.

James, *angrily*: This' how I talk, man!

Ron didn't avert his eyes, or flinch. After a long pause, James conceded.

James: Okay, fine. What time ya' want me here?

Ron did not answer.

James: Okay, what time *do* you want me here?

Ron: Seven a.m.

James: What!?

Ron: I'll have coffee for you if you drink it.

James: You got Coke?

Ron: I'll get some. See you in the morning, James.

Chapter 5

The next morning

Ron is standing at Olivia's front door.

Olivia, *whispering*: Come on in Ron. *Ron enters.* He's still sleeping. I did what you said and didn't get him up. I heard his alarm go off three or four times, but I haven't seen him yet.

Ron, *also quietly*: Mind if I go in and wake him up?

Olivia, *hesitantly*: I haven't had a chance to clean his room.

Ron: Why do you clean his room?

Olivia: Well, when I can't take the smell anymore, I have to take some action!

Ron, *laughing*: Oh, I'm not saying that his room shouldn't be clean, just wondering why you should be the one to clean it.

Olivia: Well, I don't know how I'd get him to clean it himself. He just doesn't seem to care.

Ron: Can I go back there and wake him up?

Olivia: Sure.

Ron walked through a house. It was not immaculate, but neat and clean. Olivia had a good sense of style and was a good housekeeper. Ron thought about how hard it must be to balance that with raising two boys and working a nursing job and a weekend accounting job. No wonder she often looked exhausted.

Olivia pointed to his room. The door was closed and locked. Ron knocked forcefully and waited. James assumed it was his little brother.

James: Come in here if you want a beatin'.

Ron: Okay, open the door.

A shuffle and scurry came from inside.

James, *opening the door and squinting against the light*: Oh hey … er … Mr. Powers! Am I late?

James went back to the bedside and looked at his alarm clock—7:25 a.m.

James: Mom! I'm sorry. I don't know why she didn't get me up.

Ron: Why would she?

James: She always does.

Ron: Well, she isn't going to anymore. Come on, you're late.

James: Okay, just let me get dressed.

James had sweatpants on and no shirt. Ron walked out and headed to the front door.

Ron: You have five minutes to be in my yard.

With that he disappeared. James managed to get into a t-shirt and made it to the yard in less than a minute.

Ron: How can you stand to have your room like that?

James: Oh, it's Saturday. Wait until this afternoon. You should see it then.

Ron: I told your mom she should stop cleaning your room.

James: What? Why?

Ron: James, you're old enough to clean up your own messes. A four-year-old is old enough to clean up his room. I understand that no one has ever made you take responsibility for your stuff before, but it's time you started.

Your mother works two jobs to support your family. What do you do to help? *He paused as if he expected an answer, but he didn't wait for one.* When was the last time you thanked her for her hard work? *He paused again.* I promised your mother and the judge that I would try to teach you some responsibility. It's time you start pulling your own weight.

James: *James thought this guy was as intimidating as T.* Okay, Mr. Powers. *He was wondering if juvenile center would have been easier.*

Ron: Don't come late again. *As they walked around the corner of the house to the back yard, Ron's scolding evaporated.* I think you've met my son, Jerry. *Ron had been firm, but he obviously wasn't angry.*

Jerry: Hey, James. I think we had P.E. together last year.

James. Yeah. Hey.

James picked up his rake. Jerry showed him how to use it and where they were piling the leaves while Ron went inside to cook breakfast for their morning break. At 9 a.m. Ron called the boys in and served eggs, pancakes, and Coca Cola.

The three of them worked around the yard for the rest of the morning and then stopped for a late lunch. Ron kept telling the boys how much he appreciated their help and what a good job they were doing. This was an exaggeration at first, as James wasn't working very hard. But by the end of the day, James was working as hard as Jerry and Ron, and he felt good about it. Ron playfully slapped them both on the back.

Ron: Men, very nice job today. I'm proud of you.

Ron handed James $50. James looked at it, knowing he could have made this in ten minutes working for T. But this was different—it felt satisfying.

James: You need me back tomorrow?

Ron: No, James, on Sundays we go to church. You're welcome to come with us.

James: No thanks. Do you want me to come Monday after school?

Ron: That'll be great, James. *Then he made deliberate eye contact and put his hand on James's shoulder.* Thank you again for your help today. You did a great job.

James was thinking: "*This guy is tough, but he seems to really care. I wonder why since Mom said Mr. Powers isn't getting paid to be a mentor.*"

Chapter 6

The following Monday

In Ron's kitchen, James noticed his own reflection in the mirror on the wall and tried to give the "Ron stare-down." But he knew that he just looked silly. He thought, "How does Mr. Powers do that?"

Ron, *entering the room*: Good afternoon, James. Are you ready to take it up a notch today?

James: What do you mean?

Ron: I have a fence that needs some boards replaced. Ever done anything like that?

James: Nope.

Ron: Well, there's a first time for everything. Ready?

James: Let's do this. Where's Jerry?

Ron: Jerry had work today, so we won't see him unless we're still working at seven o'clock.

James: You gonna feed me?

Ron: Of course. It's Taco Monday!

James: That sounds good.

Ron: Okay, let's get started. James, why don't you come over here and I'll show you how to work this hammer.

He showed James how to set the claws of the hammer under the head of the nail and pry it out.

Ron: Now you try it.

He expected it to be awkward for James the first few times, but James caught on quickly.

Ron: Very good, son.

A wave of something came over James when Ron called him "son." He was unprepared for the warmth in his chest at the word, but he was also uncomfortable.

James: Thank you. *Then he immediately thought, "No. Keep the man a safe distance. If you trust people, they hurt you. Don't let him in."*

Ron: Now go around and pull out the nails from all the boards that look somewhat rotten like this, and we'll stack the boards over here. Boards like this (pointing to one) are okay to keep if they are solid.

It was plain to James which boards were to be replaced and he got to work. Then Ron showed James how to nail the new boards in place. They finished around dinner time. The sliding door opened, and Jackie emerged.

Jackie, *yelling*: Taco Monday!

Ron raised an eyebrow at James and tilted his head toward the kitchen to invite him in.

James, *feeling torn between free food and letting Ron get too close*: I think I have to go.

Ron noticed James had pulled away, but he didn't know why.

Ron: Okay, James. Hang on a minute. Wind up this cord and put that stuff over behind the garage. I'll be right back.

Ron disappeared inside and came back two minutes later with a check and a Coke, handing both to James.

Ron: Here you go, James, for today.

James: Whoa! This is almost as much as last time, and we worked fewer hours.

Ron: More skill requires more pay. James, you're gifted. If you'll come back Saturday, I've got plenty of projects … 7 a.m.?

James, *seemingly a foot taller*: I'll see you then!

James headed through the gate to his own house, looking at the check in his hand. Ron watched him go. Then he turned and went inside to the smell of Taco Monday.

Chapter 7

A couple weeks later

Olivia: Ron, you know I have been really uncomfortable with how much you are pushing James to work.

Ron, *defensively*: Well, Olivia, you asked me to help him, and this is something I think will help him.

Olivia: No, that's not where I'm going. I want to tell you what happened at work today.

Ron, *softer*: Oh, I'm sorry.

Olivia: I had a patient who had *real* money, you know what I mean? I could tell by her clothes, perfume, jewelry, and the way she talked. She started telling me about all her family trouble. At first, I thought, "Honey, you have no room to complain … you've obviously got money." We did not grow up in the same neighborhood, but the more she talked, the more I realized how similar our situations were … except for the money. *She laughed.*

Her husband was very successful in business. When he died, he left a large amount of money for the kids in some kind of trust, or something like that. I didn't understand it all. But anyway, she felt like since her husband has been gone her son was starting to disrespect her. He was treating her less like a mother and more like a vending machine. She actually said that!

Ron: That's too bad.

Olivia: Yeah. The trouble is that her son has no sense of responsibility. He not only spends everything he can from the trust, but he's also deep in debt with a bunch of credit cards. He never thanks her for anything. He's careless with his stuff. If he breaks something, or loses it, he just goes out and buys another one. And she thinks he is starting to get into drugs. I was sitting there thinking, she shouldn't just be giving him money for nothing. It's spoiling him. He doesn't appreciate that someone had to work for all that money. This boy needs a job so he can understand the value of things.

She paused. Ron, I get it now.

Ron was trying to convert his, "I told you so" smile into an "I'm happy for you" smile.

Olivia: You saw me spoiling my boys the same way. I don't have that kind of money, but I was doing the same thing.

Then James came home from your place a couple weeks ago beaming. He told me how much money he made and how you thought he had done such a good job. He really felt good about what he had done. I haven't seen him that excited in a long time. He couldn't stop talking about it.

Then, the other day he did something he's never done before … ever.

Ron: What was that?

Olivia: He thanked me for all my hard work and gave me a hug. I melted right there on the spot.

She stopped to wipe the tears from her eyes. Then I got to thinking, he got that from you. Maybe I need to trust that you know what you're doing with him. He needs a man to teach him how to be a man.

She apologized with her smile, and he accepted it with his own smile.

Ron: Thank you.

Olivia: I can tell he is starting to feel better about himself.

Ron: James is good with his hands.

Olivia: Oh yeah, he's good with his hands alright! *They both laughed at her joke.*

Ron: No, Olivia, he is really good with his hands. I think he is going to work with his hands someday, but .... *He stopped.*

Olivia: But what?

Ron: I think he's ready for a regular job.

Olivia: It's okay, he can look for a job.

Ron let out a sigh.

Olivia: Ron, thanks for pushing me on this, but respectfully. And thanks for waiting until I was ready. I feel like you are showing James a good example of respect. There wasn't much of that in the neighborhood where I grew up. A lot of fear ... a lot of anger ... not much respect.

Ron: You're welcome.

She went to give him a hug of appreciation, then started to pull back because she thought that might be inappropriate. But it was too late, he embraced her spontaneously. It was enough to bring a few more tears to her eyes.

Chapter 8

That Friday (where our story began)

Shawn: You know what? I gotta go. I'll be seein' you, James. Have fun bein' a good boy.

Shawn was his oldest friend, and James wished he could make him understand his tight spot.

Later that same day James was walking home from school and a car pulled up and stopped next to him. James could tell out of the corner of his eye who it was.

T: Hey, young blood, I ain't seen you around. Why don't you get in?

James: I'm good.

T: I'm not gonna ask you twice.

He heard a click and saw a gun pointing out the window at him. James was trying to stay calm, but he was afraid T could hear his heart pounding. He could hardly think.

T: You know what this means, young blood?

Someone in the closest house pulled her curtains together and walked away from the window. James didn't know it, but she called 911.

James was frozen in time. Should he run? He'd known T long enough to know this might not be a bluff. Would he die today? Should he get in the car? What would his mother say if he went back to the gang? What would Mr. Powers say? Why did he care what Mr. Powers would say? He felt fear and anger rising. He knew he had to decide quickly or else.

But before he could even finish his thought, he was interrupted by a violent crash. James saw everything in slow motion. T's head and body bounced from the seat to the steering wheel and back. Then he slumped back down into the seat holding his bloody nose. The gun fell onto the pavement.

James looked back to see what hit T's car, and he saw a Ford Mustang Boss 351 with Ron Powers at the wheel looking almost as dazed as T.

Now Ron was unbuckling and getting out. James watched him walk up to T's window and wait until T opened his eyes and looked up. When he did, what he saw glaring back at him was "the stare." Ron's eyes bore into him as he grabbed him by the shirt and pulled him up close.

Ron: Listen, punk. This is the last time you will ever talk to this young man. Do you understand? DO YOU UNDERSTAND?!

T: Yeah, man!

Ron, *softer*: Do you need me to call someone?

T didn't know if this was a sincere offer for help, or if it was a threat. Neighbors were looking out their windows. He jerked the car into gear and drove off before the police could arrive. When they got there, Ron showed them the gun and gave them a full report. The policeman joked that this was the first time someone admitted to hitting another car where he didn't issue a ticket.

Then Ron and James walked back to Ron's car. It was still drivable, so James got in and they started toward home.

Ron: You okay?

James: Huh? Oh, yeah … wait, are *you* okay?

Ron: I think so.

James: Sorry about your car.

Ron: Cars can be fixed. *After a pause.* Do you want to talk about anything?

James, *feeling emotionally and mentally overwhelmed*: Not really.

James was doing some deep thinking. He had enjoyed belonging to T's gang. T had always spoken nicely to James and made him feel welcome. And being part of a gang made him feel powerful. Kids at school were treating him with respect, maybe fear. But now he knew if he ever crossed T, the belonging was over, and all that came with it.

Ron, on the other hand, came across harshly sometimes, but James knew this man cared for him and wanted his best. He felt safe with him, but how could he trust a man he hardly knew? James had a hard decision to make. They drove the rest of the way in silence.

Ron, *pulling into the driveway*: Seven o'clock tomorrow morning?

James, *with his mind still swirling*: I have to think about it.

Chapter 9

Saturday, 6:59 a.m., in Ron's kitchen.

James, *drinking a Coke*: So, why did you hit T's car?

Ron, *drinking coffee from his NASCAR mug*: I noticed you were walking down the sidewalk, and I was getting ready to pull up and offer you a ride. Then I saw the other car stop, and I saw the gun pointed at you. I didn't have time to think. I just instinctively hit the gas and slammed his car.

James: But that's your favorite car. Now it's a mess.

Ron: You can replace car parts. You can't replace people. James, you are way more valuable than an old car. I'm just glad God had me in the right place at the right time.

The wheels in James's head could almost be heard above the long quiet pause.

Ron: What are you spending your money on, James?

James: Whatever I want.

Ron: Like what?

James: Like food, clothes, games, videos.

Ron: Have you ever thought about saving some of it?

James: What for?

Ron: You will want things that cost more than one paycheck, and if you don't save up, you won't be able to buy them.

James: Like what?

Ron: Like a car.

James: Huh. I never thought about that.

Ron: That's why I'm asking.

A few weeks later Ron brought up the subject again.

Ron: James, what are you doing with your money now?

James: Nothing. Just saving it.

Ron: Glad to hear you're saving it. Where are you saving it?

James: In the bank.

Ron already knew from his bank records that the last couple checks hadn't been cashed.

Ron: What bank do you use?

James panicked. What was the name of that bank he passed on the way to school? He couldn't remember.

Ron: James, you need to know that there is never any reason to lie to me. Do you have a bank account?

James, *after a long pause*: I don't … sorry.

Ron resisted the urge to make it easy on him.

James: I just don't. I don't want you to think I am a stupid kid who doesn't know anything.

Ron: You never need worry about what I'm going to think about you, James. I already know you're a thief.

James looked up at Ron and saw his straight face crack into a grin.

James, *relieved as the tension deflates*: Oh, so you've got jokes. At least I'm not … never mind.

Ron: Go ahead. *They were both smiling and getting warmed up.*

James: Nah, I know you're probably sensitive about your plaid underwear.

Both laughed for a good half a minute.

Ron: Tell you what, after we finish working today, let's talk with your mom about opening a bank account. We'll probably need her to sign.

James: Really? That's cool.

They went outside to power wash the algae off the walls of a storage shed and tackle a list of chores. Jerry came out when he got home from sleeping over at a friend's house, and they made short work of the projects.

Chapter 10

That afternoon

Olivia was in Ron and Jackie's living room.

Ron, *patiently*: What's making it feel so hard for you, Olivia?

The boys were outside eating a snack. Ron and Jackie were sitting in the living room with Olivia. Olivia didn't like the idea. It was like her resistance against James working.

Jackie: Olivia, tell us what you're thinking.

Olivia, *not even able to look at them, bore great distress in her face*: It's just that … I really don't know, Jackie. It was hard for me to let James work. I want to be able to provide for him, but I can see that it was the right thing. He's obviously doing much better, and the sense of pride that he has in his work is good. I sometimes have to trust in something besides my feelings as a mother, and that's almost impossible.

Jackie: I completely understand, Olivia. My maternal instinct is to nurture them and protect them from everything hard.

Olivia: That's right. It's hard not to beat myself up for the choices I've made regarding their father. But it is what it is.

Ron, I'm glad you helped me see that James needs to work, but I don't want him to get his own bank account yet. I mean, why? He can cash his checks when he gets them. Why does he need a bank account?

Ron, *looking sympathetically*: Olivia, the sense of pride and maturity that you've seen in him since he started making money will deepen if James can have his own bank account. James will be grown before you know it, and he'll need to have experience saving money and keeping a checking account.

Olivia: But that's just it. I don't … *then slowly and quietly,* I don't want him to grow up.

Ron and Jackie looked at each other knowingly.

Ron: Can you say that again, Olivia?

Olivia was quiet. She was thinking about what she'd just said.

Olivia: When I find out he's been acting crazy and robbing stores, I think, "Why can't he just stay my baby? Why do they have to grow up and become criminals?"

She started to cry.

Jackie: Olivia, I think you know deep down that this isn't the way. You have to allow him to become a man and that is risky.

Olivia kept crying. Ron could see that these fears were deep-rooted, but he was determined to do what he'd signed up to do.

Ron: You asked me to take this on and be a mentor. I'll never be able to replace his dad, but I can offer some of the things a dad would offer. This is one of them—to push him and help him take on more responsibility. Let him do this, Olivia, or he will end up a thirty-year-old child living in your house … or worse.

Ron knew he was pushing. Jackie looked tense but supportive of them both. She'd seen Ron like this many times, and she admired the way her husband managed to say hard things with love and kindness.

Olivia seemed to stare at him for a long time, but finally had to look away.

Olivia, *sighing heavily*: I know you're right, Ron. Okay, let's get him a bank account.

Ron smiled, and Jackie put a nurturing hand on Olivia's shoulder.

Jackie: I'm proud of you, Olivia. I know this is hard.

Olivia, *meekly*: Ron, you say James would be living at home at thirty. Well, to me, that's not a bad thing. I really love my kids and want them around. I *need* them. But I can see now that if I truly love James, I'll have to teach him how to stand on his own. *More tears.*

Jackie: I am so amazed at you Olivia. I can see how hard this is, but I can see you want what's best for James.

Ron: Maybe you can take him to the bank on Monday?

Olivia: Well … actually, I was hoping you could come too. It seems fitting to me.

Ron, *impressed again*: I'd be happy to, Olivia.

Chapter 11

A week later

Ron sat in his living room reading. His feet were up, and his glasses were on the edge of his nose when James glanced through the window of the front door. He was getting used to seeing Ron that way. He knocked.

Ron: Come on in, kid. Looking spiffy!

James: I look fresh. I don't know about *spiffy*.

They both laughed.

Ron: Are you off to your interview?

James: Yeah.

Ron: Good deal! Which job is this? The movie theater?

James: Nah, they didn't have enough hours. It's the pizza place.

Ron: Oh, right. Roma's. That place has been around a long time.

James: Yeah. I get to sample the merchandise when I go.

Ron: Do they pay you in pizza?

James, *chuckling*: No, but I heard they let us take a pizza home if someone orders one and doesn't pick it up.

Ron: Wow! Well, you're at the age where you can probably get away with a pizza a day. What time is the interview?

James: It's in fifteen minutes.

Ron: You better get going then!

James: See you later.

Ron: James, you are going to do a great job!

James: Thank you, Mr. Powers.

Ron, *as James was closing the door*: Oh James, did you see the news about T?

James: I don't watch the news, really.

Ron: They tried to rob another store last week.

James: I knew that was coming. The cameras were supposed to be out.

Ron: Well, the cameras might have been out, but an off-duty cop was in the store at the same time they held up the cashier.

James: What happened?

Ron: Between the weapons and drugs they found in his car, I don't think we are going to see T again for a while.

James, *a look of relief, then concern, crossing his face*: Did they say anything about Shawn?

Ron: No, they said one of the robbers got away. Would that have been him?

James: Probably.

Chapter 12

The next day

James: Mr. Powers!

Ron turned around. He had been watering his flowers.

Ron: James! How goes it?

James: I got it!

Ron played dumb by giving him a quizzical look.

James: The job at Roma's!

Ron couldn't stop a big smile from spreading across his face. He knew this was big milestone. He gave James a hug. James knew his mother loved him, but it especially felt good to have the approval and encouragement of the older man.

However, James stiffened and pulled away. He didn't want to be hurt again, like he had been when his father left.

Ron, *unphased*: James that's great. I am so glad for you. Tell me all about the interview.

James: Well, I went in and at first it was really awkward. Everyone was just looking at me and thinking, "He thinks he can work here? Who does he think he is?"

Ron, *laughing*: I doubt they were actually thinking that.

James, *laughing along*: Maybe not, but that's how it felt. A girl named Gretchen went and got the manager, and he came out to meet me. He was really cool. He shook my hand.

Ron: And you offered him a limp fish handshake?

James: Nope! I did it just like you showed me. I looked him in the eye, and I shook his hand firmly. Maybe a little too firmly.

Ron: That's fine.

James: Anyway, we sat down and started talking. He asked me why I wanted to work there, and what I wanted to do when I grew up.

Ron: What did you say?

James: I said I wanted to make some money and get some work experience. I said I didn't really know what I wanted to do, but I knew I wanted to work. I told him I like working and being useful. He asked me if I had ever made pizzas before.

Ron: Have you?

James: No, and I wanted to lie, but I didn't.

Ron: I'm glad.

James: Then he showed me around. I started to get a good feeling like maybe he was going to hire me right there. But he said he had two more interviews, that he had already interviewed two other people, but that he was looking to fill two positions. Doing the math, I started to get worried. Five interviews, two jobs. Not good.

Ron: But I guess you were one of the two!

James: I guess so! I'm pretty amped.

Ron: When do you start?

James: Next week.

Ron: Amazing. Let's celebrate!

Ron got two Cokes out of the fridge.

James: I didn't think you drank that stuff.

Ron: Only on special occasions.

Chapter 13

The next week at Roma's

Paul: And that's it. Once your pizza's done, start another one.

James: Okay. I think I got it.

Paul: Let me see you try.

James pulled off a ball of dough and weighed it. It came up a little short, but James figured that was okay and he started to roll it out.

Paul: Uh, uh, James. It has to be exactly the right weight. Go ahead and add to it. Consistency is really important.

James: Why is that?

Paul: Well, how would you feel if you went to a restaurant and got something that you really loved, only to come back and order it a second time, but it was smaller, or not as good?

James: I would be disappointed.

Paul: Would you go back?

James: I'd think twice.

Paul: There you go.

James: Okay, so 16 ounces exactly.

James pulled off a few small pieces to add until he got it right, then he started to roll it out. He had to start over a few times until at last he had a circular pizza crust of 14 inches.

James: When do I get to spin it around and throw it in the air?

Paul stares at him deadpan. James becomes uncomfortable and wonders if he's in trouble. Just then Paul breaks and starts laughing.

Paul: We'll see about that after you can make a circular pizza crust on the first try for a while.

As the shift went on, James noticed something.

James: You really seem to care about all this.

Paul: I do.

James: I'm guessing you want to own your own pizza place someday?

Paul: No, not even remotely. I'm only going to be here for four more months. Then I leave for medical school.

James: Oh wow! You're going to be a doctor?

Paul: That's the plan.

James: I don't get it. Why do you care so much about this job?

Paul: Because I am paid to.

James: Yeah, but it's just a pizza place.

Paul became very serious.

Paul: James, nobody starts out doing work that they necessarily love. For most people, their first jobs are grueling and monotonous—bagging groceries all day, loading boxes, mowing lawns, stuff like that. But it's how you do those jobs that determine the next level.

James: What do you mean? By-the-way, do you know Ron Powers?

Paul: No, who is that?

James: Oh, just my neighbor. You remind me of him.

Paul, *grinning*: He must be a real stud. *They both smiled.*

Mr. Wallace owns this place. He trusts me to do a job. Any job that anyone entrusts to me is important to me. It's not that I think I can save lives making pizza, but I do believe that how I go about my work here will make me into the kind of man I want to be going to medical school, which will lead me to become the kind of doctor I want to be.

James: Who did you learn all this from?

Paul: Honestly, probably the military.

James: You were in the military? I'll bet you could kill me right here!

They both laughed.

Paul: I was a medic. But in basic training we were taught to pay careful attention to little details that most people would think were unimportant. Like, we had to fold our underwear and stack it so perfectly that it looked like a ream of paper. Seems pointless, right?

James, *sarcastically*: You could say that.

Paul: But how you do one thing leads to how you are going to do another. If you are careful and pay attention to detail in one area, you will likely do the same in other areas. I want to do everything to the best of my ability, because, well … that's what a man does.

James: Are you sure you don't know Ron Powers?

Chapter 14

Five weeks later.

Ron: James, I've been curious about how things are going at Roma's. It seems like you're getting to work almost every day.

James: Yeah, Paul seems to like me a lot, and I have been really liking it there.

Ron: He seems like a good egg.

James: A what?

Ron: Never mind.

James: Mr. Powers, can I talk to you?

Ron: Sure.

James: Once I got the bank account and had a way to cash my checks, I started spending my money like crazy. I don't even know what all I bought, some magazines, new clothes, snacks at school. I can't believe how fast it went. I worked for two weeks and spent it all in a couple days. Then, I decided I wouldn't spend a penny, so I just put my last paycheck in the bank. I keep going back and forth.

Ron: Well, that's good.

James: But now I am afraid to spend anything. Whenever I see something, I want to buy it. I can't help but think, "I have to make pizzas, sweep floors, clean counters for four hours to buy that. No thanks."

Ron, *laughing*: That's a good way to think of it, James. You are learning the value of your time.

James: Ha! I don't feel very valuable if I'm making minimum wage!

Ron: For now. This will help you see what kind of job you want to have when you're grown up. This work experience, even at minimum wage, is valuable.

James: Paul told me the same thing last week. But what do I do? I don't really know how to handle money.

Ron: It's time you learned my rule.

James: It figures you would have a rule. What is it?

Ron: Only go 55.

Even considering Ron's car hobby, James expected Ron could not have been talking about driving, so he waited.

Ron: When I was your age, my dad taught me to divide my money into four piles whenever I got paid: giving, taxes, saving, and spending.

James: So, four equal piles?

Ron: No, not equal. It's really up to you, but here's what I recommend. Put 10 percent aside for giving.

James: Giving to what?

Ron: To some person who needs it more than you, or to a charity that is helping people.

James: Why would I do that?

Ron: There's an old saying, "It is more blessed to give than to receive."

James, *skeptically*: Sounds like something a beggar would write on cardboard.

Ron, *laughing*: Maybe so. But it's true. When we give, we benefit even more than the person we are trying to help.

James: How so?

Ron: I can't explain it. But if you try it, you'll see what I mean.

James, *raising a dubious eyebrow and nodding slowly*: Okay.

Ron: You don't need a tax pile for your Roma's income since they probably take it out of your check, but anything you make working for me, you should probably set aside 20 percent for taxes.

James: Man, that's a lot!

Ron: Yes, it is. I can explain how that works when we file your tax return next year. You may or may not make enough to owe taxes, but in case you do, you don't want to have to come up with it on short notice.

James: And then you said save and spend.

Ron: Saving is 15 percent, and spending is 55 percent.

James: If I make $100, I only get to keep $55?

Ron: You get to *spend* $55. You only *keep* what you save.

James, *smiling*: That's true.

Ron: And if you invest it, you'll see it grow. We can talk about that as well. If you have a plan like this, you'll be less worried about your spending because you'll know you won't spend all of it.

James: What if I want to save more?

Ron: You can, and right now while you have no bills to pay, you probably should.

James: Thanks Mr. Powers. I feel better having a plan.

Chapter 15

Two months later

James looked forward to the twenty hours per week he spent at the pizzeria. At first, he was a little distant from the other employees, but now they had become like family. They knew each other well and worked together well.

There was Gretchen. She was his age, the only daughter of a single mom. She was friendly, but serious and quiet most of the time. She was the hardest worker of the team, taking the shift of anyone who couldn't come in for whatever reason.

There was Simon, a kid with long dark hair who loved music, video games, and building computers. Every cent he made at the place went into those hobbies.

There was Isaiah, a short, nineteen-year-old who looked like he was younger than James. He seemed very smart and could be hilarious. His father worked at a bank and his mother was a schoolteacher. He was old enough to work late, so he often worked the closing shift.

And of course, his manager, Paul. James really liked him and looked up to him. Paul seemed to like James as well.

Paul: Hey James, remember what we were going to do today?

James: Yeah, inventory. Can't I make pizzas? I don't really like bookwork.

Paul: I understand. But you have the potential to manage this place someday. To do that, you'll need to know how to do inventory.

James, *feeling surprised and complimented*: All right.

Just then, one of their regular customers came in.

Jenny, *a middle-aged woman with a friendly expression*: Hi Paul. Hi James.

Paul and James, *together*: Hi Jenny.

Jenny: Is it ready?

Paul: It is.

Jenny: I knew I could count on you guys.

James looked at Paul and smiled. James was ringing up her order.

James: A medium Hawaiian and a two liter of diet?

Jenny: Oh! Skip the Diet Coke. I still have some in my fridge.

James: Okay. That'll be $13.75.

Jenny: There you go, James. Keep the change.

She had handed him a ten and a five.

James: Thank you.

He put the money into the cash register and took out one dollar to put in his pocket. Then he picked up Jenny's pizza from under the heat lamp and handed it to her.

Paul: Have a nice day, Jenny.

Jenny: You too, goodbye. *She walked out the door.*

James looked sideways at Paul, who winked at him.

Paul: You only took $1 out of the register, but your tip was $1.25.

James: Yeah. I don't like messing with change.

Paul: So, you just rounded down to the nearest dollar?

James: Or up, whichever is closer.

Paul: Whoa! Two problems, James.

James: Like what?

Paul: One, when you round up, you are taking money from the store that doesn't belong to you.

James: But it's just a small amount.

Paul, *thinking about what to say*: What if you were taking $100 a day out of the register?

James: That would be stealing. I don't do that anymore.

Paul: What about $20 a day?

James: Same thing.

Paul: What about $5?

James: What's your point?

Paul: It's not the amount, it's who the money belongs to.

James: But I figure it works out over time. Sometimes up and sometimes down.

Paul: That's the second problem. When I run the register report at the end of the day, everything is supposed to balance. It's usually off by a little bit. But it's never way off. Now I know why. So far, this month, we're down about $13.

James: Well, Simon does it too.

Paul: If you want to put the change in the cup by the register, that's up to you. But you should never take money that belongs to the store. Not only is it wrong. It throws off the books. And there's something else, it's also a reflection on me and my management. I'm accountable for every dollar.

James felt defensive. He thought Paul was making a big deal out of nothing. But, just as his anger was starting to inflate, a sharp thought came along and popped it. He thought of complaining to Mr. Powers and knew Mr. Powers would agree with Paul. He was embarrassed to admit it, but he knew in his gut Paul was right.

James: Do you want me to pay it back?

Paul: No, but I want you to get Simon. I need to talk to him, too.

Chapter 16

11:15 p.m. on a Saturday night, three months later

Gretchen was clearing out the last dishwasher load of silverware and cups.

Gretchen: James, you're really coming out of your shell. You were so shy when you started.

Paul: *He* was shy?

James looked quizzically at them both.

Gretchen: What?

Paul: James, she didn't even speak to the first person she checked out. She opened her mouth, but nothing came out. Then she just stared at the cash register like it was written in a foreign language. The customer was nice about it, but it was *awkward!*

Gretchen: Aw, come on!

Paul, *grinning*: But look at how far you've come. Now you make everyone feel welcomed, and you are the official Queen of the Cash Register.

Gretchen bowed her head slightly and held out her hand as if she expected them to kiss it. Both Paul and James looked at her a moment before bursting out laughing.

Isaiah, and Simon, headphones on his neck, started knocking hard on the locked back door.

Paul, *opening the door*: Get in here.

The employees made an epic extra-large pizza every Saturday night after closing. It was Paul's idea, and Mr. Wallace okayed it months earlier. It had been a tradition ever since.

Simon: Anchovies, anchovies, anchovies!

Everyone else: NOOOOOO!

Paul: Simon, do you know how many anchovy pizzas I've sold in the four years I've worked here?

Simon: Ummmm, thousands?

Paul: Maybe ten. Nine of them were to you! I've sold more SPAM pizzas than I have anchovy.

Gretchen: Gross!

They all chipped in ideas for tonight's gargantuan pizza but settled for dividing it into parts so everyone could have what they wanted.

Paul: Tonight is a special occasion.

James: Why?

Paul: Well, this will be my last Saturday night at Roma's.

Everyone was shocked.

Simon: Duuuude! What? Why?!
Paul: I start med school in two months, and I am moving next week. Tuesday is my last day. This is a little sooner than I expected.

Isaiah: Why so fast?

Paul: I found a good, short-term job near the school where I can work a lot of hours before classes start.

James felt like someone had punched him in the gut. He hid his disappointment, but it was difficult.

Gretchen: What are we going to do without a manager?

Paul: Mr. Wallace has already hired someone. I recommended James, but Mr. Wallace's nephew needed a job, and I guess he's worked in other pizza places. He'll be the new manager.

Isaiah: Are you going to tell him about Saturday nights?

Paul: Sure.

Paul had dropped hints to James about managing someday, but James didn't take these comments very seriously. Obviously, Paul did. It was an encouraging surprise to find out Paul had recommended him, but a disappointment to find out it didn't matter.

They all had an uneasy feeling about Paul leaving. Everyone but James was able to shake it off and enjoy the night. James felt sick. He told himself he didn't care. That way, it might not bother him as much. But it didn't work. He really admired Paul, the way he approached life, the way he treated everyone with respect. He knew he would miss Paul deeply.

Chapter 17

The next Tuesday

Paul: That's pretty much it. Do you want me to show you anything else?

Paul was showing the new manager, Neil, everything he thought he'd need to know.

Neil: No, man. I've done this before.

Paul: Okay. Well, my shift isn't over for three more hours. So, I'll be around if you need anything.

Neil: That's all right. I don't need you. You can just take your stuff and leave.

Paul hoped Neil hadn't meant that to sting, but it did.

James came in the front door to begin his shift.

Paul: Hey, James, meet Neil. He's the new manager.

Neil: Hey.

James, *reaching to shake hands*: Nice to meet you, Neil.

Neil, *looking James up and down with an unapproving look and with a crooked smile*: You too, Jimmy.

James disliked him immediately.

Chapter 18

A week later

Olivia stopped over to thank Ron for all he and Jackie had been doing. Not only had Ron been employing James, but he was also teaching him how to fix the car, and they had invited her family over for many evening meals together.

Ron: You are most welcome. I'm really enjoying getting to know James. I especially enjoy it when he gives me a hard time.

Olivia: Is he being disrespectful?

Ron: Not at all. Olivia, do you have a minute to talk?

Olivia: I need to get supper started, but it can wait a few minutes.

Ron: I have a question for you.

Olivia: Yeah?

Ron: Do you like your work?

Olivia: No, not really.

Ron: Why not? Or maybe I should ask, what would you really love to do?

Olivia: I trained to be a nurse, so I figure that's it. I just do what I need to do to get by. I have two jobs and I don't really enjoy either one of them, for the most part.

Ron: You have really sacrificed for your two boys, and worked very hard, but you seem to talk more about your weekend job than about nursing. I was thinking how I would sure like to see you enjoy your work.

Olivia: I never thought of work as something to enjoy. I just saw it as my ticket out of our old neighborhood. If I got a degree, then I could get a job and move to a better neighborhood. Then we'd be okay.

Ron: Olivia, I believe God made you to do a specific kind of work.

Olivia: You remind me of my grandma.

Ron, *laughing*: I've never been accused of that before.

Olivia: I mean you and Jackie are people of faith.

Ron: Yes, we are. Neither one of us grew up that way, but we are now.

Olivia: For me, it's the other way around. My grandma took me to church when I was little, but I've drifted away from church and God and all that.

Ron: Hmm.

Olivia: So, what were you going to say about work?

Ron: When you are doing what God made you to do, it doesn't feel like work—it's a pleasure. Don't get me wrong, it's still frustrating or boring at times, but there is just something about finding what you were made to do, and doing it, that is really satisfying.

Olivia: It's funny you should mention that I talk more about my weekend job than nursing. I do actually enjoy a couple parts of my weekend job, but other parts I really hate.
Ron: For example?

Olivia: Well, I started working there on weekends when I was in school, so I know the company very well. I have to fill in these tax forms from time to time. I hate that. But I also keep track of all kinds of information and run reports every month for my boss. I love to look at the information and see what it means.

Ron: What do you mean by that?

Olivia: It's obvious what these reports tell us about the company, but no one else seems to see it quite as clearly as I do. I make suggestions about what we need to change, and my boss is starting to listen to me more and more. I think my ideas are helping us save money and grow as a company.

Ron: How does that make you feel?

Olivia: I never thought about it much, but it makes me feel pretty good.

Ron: Do you enjoy nursing?

Olivia: I did at first. But healthcare keeps changing. We spend less and less time with patients and more and more time documenting information. When I started nursing, I thought I could really make a difference, and I kept my weekend job for extra money. Now, I feel like I'm making more of a difference on my weekend job.

Ron: What if you spent less time nursing and more time at your weekend job?

Olivia: Actually, my boss has been asking me about that lately. But I didn't see how it could make sense, financially, so I told him, "No."

Ron: Did you tell him why you said no?

Olivia: Didn't seem important. I make less money per hour for him than I do nursing.

Ron: But it sounds like you are adding a lot of value to the company. What if he thought it was worth giving you a raise to get you to work more hours?

Olivia: You're serious, aren't you?

Ron: I am Olivia. What would it hurt to have a conversation with him? See what he has in mind?

Olivia: I guess it wouldn't hurt. I just don't think it'll amount to much. I should get home and start supper. *Pause.* I suppose I could talk to my boss.

Ron: If you do, I'll be interested to hear how that goes.

Chapter 19

The next week

Olivia: Ron and Jackie, you'll never guess what happened!

Jackie: Tell us.

Olivia: I asked my boss if we could talk. I explained what I was thinking about both jobs, and he asked me a lot of questions. He wanted to know how many hours I was working as a nurse, and how much money I was making. He did some calculations on a pad of paper, then offered me more money than I am making now at both jobs combined if I would work for him full time.

Ron: Wow, Olivia, that's great!

Olivia: That's not the best part. I will have weekends off so I can spend more time with the boys.

Jackie: We are so happy for you.

Ron: Yes, we are. What do you think you'll do?

Olivia: I can't believe this is real. I think I am going to quit nursing and accept his offer. The timing's too incredible. He wanted me to take on more work for some time, but I kept shrugging it off, so he was going to hire someone else. It won't cost him any more to bring me on full time than he was going to pay for me and the new person anyway. And … guess what else?

Ron: What?

Olivia: He found someone else to do the tax forms!

Ron, *giving Olivia a high five*: Aren't you glad you talked to him?

Olivia: Ron, thanks for suggesting it. I honestly wouldn't have thought of it.

Ron: Some people think their company couldn't survive without them even though they provide very little value. Others bring substantial value to work and don't realize how much of a difference they make. I think you are the second one.

Olivia: I'm going to turn in my two weeks' notice at the hospital. I'll miss some of my co-workers, but I'm getting excited about work for the first time in a long time.

Ron: Can I draw you a picture I've drawn for my kids?

Olivia: Absolutely!

Ron, *gathering a pen and paper*: Working your way "up" is not about climbing a corporate ladder, but about climbing a pyramid.

Olivia, *winking at Jackie*: A pyramid scheme, huh?

After returning her smile, Ron outlined a pyramid, then drew three lines across it, making four levels.

Ron: Here are the assumptions behind this work pyramid:
Pay, prestige, and power can be rewarding, but will not, ultimately, bring work satisfaction. In fact, it can be like trying to satisfy a fire by throwing another log onto it. Instead of being satisfied, the fire only grows "hungrier." Just look at Wall Street pay, Hollywood prestige, and Washington, D.C., power—more is always the answer, right?

Olivia: That's for sure.

Ron: It's not about how much we make. I believe God wired each of us to do certain kinds of work. Discovering and doing this is what brings work satisfaction. *This* is success.

Olivia: Hmm.

Ron: Most of us don't know what we were made to do until we gain life experiences. And these often prepare us for the next thing. Have you heard of King David in the Bible?

Olivia, *slowly recalling*: Yesss.

Ron: First he was a shepherd, then a musician in the king's court, then a soldier, then a military commander, then he became king. He learned things doing each of these jobs that prepared him for the next job.

Olivia: I never thought of that.

Ron wrote one word in each section of the pyramid, from bottom to top, "must," "can," "enjoy," and "love,":

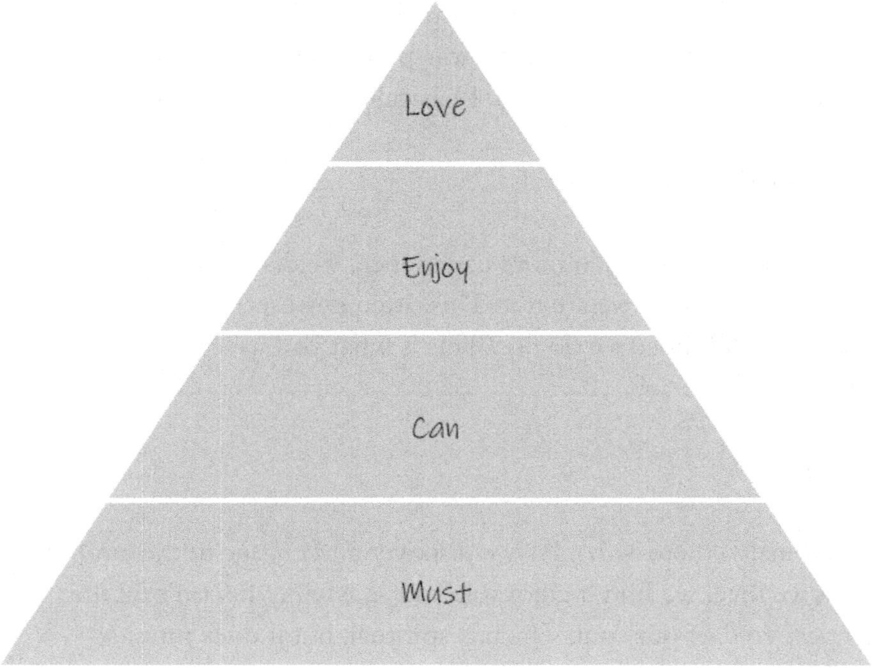

Ron: *Must.* We begin at the bottom of the work pyramid, doing what we must. In other words, we do whatever work we can find. As a child, it might be shoveling snow, mowing lawns, babysitting, etc.

Olivia: I certainly did a lot of babysitting for my brothers and sisters, but I didn't get paid very often.

Jackie: You too?

Ron, *smiling sympathetically:* Then comes *can.* We commonly move up to better opportunities because of age, experience, training, circumstances, etc. These might be jobs during college, or right out of college.

Olivia: I had a desk job at one of the dormitories during college. It was an early morning shift, so traffic was pretty light, and most people who walked by were still half asleep. I basically got paid to do homework.

Ron: Good example.

Enjoy is next. As we gain more experience, we discover the tasks we are skilled at and those we are not. This often corresponds with the tasks we enjoy, and those we do not. This is what you have just been sorting out.

Olivia: Yes.

Ron: Finally, there is *love.* As we discover and engage in the kind of work we love, we find it enjoyable and satisfying. It won't fill the deepest void of our soul, which is spiritual, but it does provide gratification to help others while doing something that seems natural to us.

Olivia: Can I have that paper? I want to show this to my boys.

Ron: Certainly.

Ron and Jackie looked at each other, and both knew what the other was thinking. They were often like that, in sync, and reading each other's minds.

Jackie: Olivia, I know you said you grew up going to church, and that you don't go anywhere now. Would you be interested in joining us in a home Bible study Thursday night? I really have a feeling you would like it.

Olivia genuinely wanted to refuse. She had had several negative experiences with church and Christians in the past. In fact, Ron and

Jackie were two of the first Christians Olivia had any good interactions with. She wanted to say no, but something stopped her.

Olivia: Thank you Jackie. I'm … sure, I'll try it. Would it be okay to invite the boys to join us? I doubt if they would be interested, but I sometimes think it would be good for the boys to do something like that.

Jackie: They're certainly welcome.

Chapter 20

A couple months later

James was counting his money when Olivia popped her head in his bedroom door.

Olivia: Hey, what are you doing?

James: Hey, Mom. I'm just counting my "give" money.

Olivia: "Give" money?

James: Yeah. Mr. Powers said I should only go 55.

Olivia: What does that mean?

James: He says I should only spend 55 percent of what I make, save 20 percent for taxes, 15 percent for savings, and 10 percent for giving away. I don't have to save 20 percent for taxes on the money I make at Roma's because they take it out of my check. And I have been putting my "save" money in the bank. But this is my "give" money.

Olivia's pride in her son swelled a bit.

Olivia: Looks like you have a good amount there.

James: Yeah, but I don't really know who or what to give it to.

Olivia: Well, when the time comes, you'll know.

James: Mr. Powers said the same thing. He said I'd need to be ready when God nudges. I don't know what that means, but I'm ready. I've got a little over $200 already.

Olivia, *impressed*: Wow, son, that's great. Can't wait to see what you end up doing with it.

Chapter 21

Two days later at Roma's

Gretchen: Look out, James!

Gretchen was moving fast through the kitchen with a high stack of pizza delivery boxes. The stack was so high she couldn't quite see where she was going.

James: Gretchen, slow down!

Just as she was opening her mouth to answer, she stumbled and sent the pile of boxes flying.

James laughed with Simon. It wasn't often that Gretchen was anything less than poised and in control. He looked at her, expecting her to laugh too. Instead, he could see she was crying. Simon felt awkward and left the kitchen.

James: Gretchen, it's no big deal. Don't worry about it. I'll help you pick these up.

Gretchen: It's not that, James. I'm just stressed out today.

With that, she put her face in her hands and cried. But she quickly pulled herself together. Gretchen had had a tough life, and she had learned to be resilient.

James: What's going on?

Gretchen, *weighing her answer*: James, it's my mom.

James knew Gretchen was raised by a single mother who had been badly treated by most of the people in her life and was very sick. He also wondered if she was an alcoholic. Gretchen had never called her that, but he figured it out from some of the comments she had made.

Gretchen: She can get into this rehab place that everyone says is the best. People really do get better there. We got some government help that pays for most of it, but we still must come up with $500. I've been saving for weeks, and I only have come up with $289 dollars. If she misses this opportunity, she won't be able to try again for six months. James, I don't know if she can make it another six months. I don't know if I can.

James felt strange suddenly. Something was happening. Was he nervous? Why did he feel so weird?

James: Did you say you need $211?

Gretchen: Yes.

James: Gretchen, can you do without me for 15 minutes? I need to get something from home.

Gretchen: What? Really?

James, *clocking out and running toward the front door with his apron still on*: Yes! I'll be right back. Don't leave. I mean. I know you won't leave, but … I'll be right back!

James got more excited with every step he took. He started jogging, then running, then sprinting. Within three minutes he had covered the four blocks to his house and was in his room, counting his "give money." He knew he had a little over $200, but he couldn't remember exactly how much.

James, *counting aloud*: $201, $202, $207, 8, 9, 10 … 11! $211! James sat down on the bed. He still had that weird feeling, but it was eclipsed by his excitement. Gretchen needed *exactly* $211 to send her mother for the treatment she needed. James had set aside *exactly* $211! This was too weird!

He would have to tell Mr. Powers what happened just as soon as he saw him again. Meanwhile, he had four blocks to cover. He sprinted all the way back to Roma's.

James, *out of breath and holding out the money to Gretchen*: Here! Take this for your mom!

Gretchen, *pushing it away in disbelief*: What? No!

James: Please! I've been waiting to *just know* who to give this money to. Mr. Powers said I would just know. My mom said the same thing. I saved *exactly* $211, and you need *exactly* $211! I know this is what it is for. Please let me do this! It's important!

Gretchen began to weep. Even though she had a huge heart herself, unfortunately, she had not experienced much generosity in her life. Her mother was kind to her, but her mother's life was a total disaster. Gretchen had been taking care of her mom since she was seven years old. There were many men in and out of their home. They ranged from indifferent to cruel. This act of love and generosity was too much. She couldn't hold back the tears. She nodded at James and then dashed to the bathroom to cry and compose herself.

While preparing for the dinner rush, James noticed that his face was hurting. He realized he was smiling really hard and must look funny. He didn't care. He was happier than he could ever remember being. Now he understood what Mr. Powers had said about being more blessed to give.

Chapter 22

A few days later

James was walking up to Roma's and came in the door. The manager, Neil, was there talking with a girl who must have just started working that day. She was pretty, so James wanted to stop and meet her. However, he didn't want to interact with Neil, so he was glad Neil's back was to him so he could sneak by quietly. Neil was rude to each worker and to some of the guests. His frequent long smoking breaks dropped the load on everyone else's shoulders. Now he sounded angry.

Neil: No, do it again.

Emma, the new girl, was flustered.

Emma: I'm sorry. Can you show me one more time?

She looked like she expected to be hit by Neil, who wore his impatience on his face.

Neil, *sighing and speaking in the voice one might use to address a bad dog*: You always start with your employee code. Then you start putting in the order. You can't put in the order until you punch in your code.

Emma's hands were shaking as she worked.

Neil, *sarcastically*: Good girl!

Emma seemed like she was ready to cry.

Neil: James!

James had been in the back where he couldn't be seen, but he had heard everything. He came up front when called.

Neil: Show Emma how to work the cash register. I'm going outside.

There was an awkward pause after he left.

James: Hi. I'm James. Your name is Emma?

Emma, *shyly*: Yeah.

James: Welcome to Roma's. Looks like you're having a great first day.

James kept a deadpan expression but couldn't keep it up and broke into a smile. Emma, at first confused, appreciated the sarcasm.

Emma: Yeah, a great first day. Thanks to Neil. He's so nice.

Emma cracked a smile, and they both laughed.

James: So, you want to learn to be world famous on the cash register. That's bold. I didn't learn the cash register until I'd been here a week. Well, lesson number one is this ….

James went on to explain the basic functions. The store was open, but it was another fifteen minutes before a customer came in. Then quite a few came all at once. James helped her through the rush. Simon and Neil were working the kitchen. James could hear Neil barking at Simon. James thought Simon was intentionally playing dumb, and it was getting under Neil's skin. He couldn't help but smile.

James was enjoying working with Emma. Later that night as he was walking home, his thoughts returned to their interaction again and again. She was petite, graceful, and beautiful. It seemed to be her eyes.

Her face looked young, but her eyes looked older. Maybe not older, but wiser. They sparkled and seemed to understand things. When he was talking with her, she was so focused on him that he would forget what he was saying. He was glad to see that he was scheduled to work with her two more times that week.

Chapter 23

A week and a half later

James, Gretchen, and Emma were in Roma's. James had been promoted to shift leader just before Paul left. Neil wasn't coming in tonight, so everyone was in high spirits.

Gretchen: We should do Saturday night this week.

The team had not done one of those since Paul left.

James went over to look at the schedule, and his face lit up.

James: Hey, we could! Neil isn't scheduled for Saturday night. He's opening and gets off at five!

Gretchen, *excited*: I'm off that night, but I'll come in.

Emma: What's Saturday night?

Gretchen: You have to come. You're scheduled to close anyway. When the restaurant closes, we make an epic pizza of some kind and just hang out. We used to do it all the time before our old manager left. The owner doesn't mind, but no one has been in the mood since "you know who" showed up.

Emma, *learning to take any chance to give James a hard time, she pointed a thumb in his direction*: This guy?

Gretchen: Oh yeah, don't tell him.

Both girls laughed.

James didn't mind. He had a good sense of humor and hoped that Emma was flirting with him.

Emma: Gretchen told me about what you did for her mom.

James's face grew hot. He didn't know why this embarrassed him, but he liked that Emma seemed impressed. James didn't know what to say, so he stared dumbly.

Emma: That was so nice.

James: Well, you see, I had the exact amount she needed, so … I just, I mean, it wasn't a big deal.

Gretchen: It was a big deal! I still can't believe it.

James, *happy to change the subject*: How is your mom doing? Does she like it there?

Gretchen: Actually, yes.

James: You seemed surprised.

Gretchen: Well, this place is supposed to be the best, but it isn't the first time she's tried rehab. She seems different this time. I don't know why, but it feels like this just might be the time she gets it together.

James: I hope so.

Gretchen: Hey James, you're basically running this place.

James: Not really.

Gretchen: Yeah, really. When are you going to call Mr. Wallace and tell him about Neil?

James: I'm not.

Gretchen: I can't stand him. I don't even like to be here when he's here.

James: I understand, but remember what Paul used to tell us? "We're a team. We have each other's back." He wouldn't let us talk bad about anyone who wasn't here.

Gretchen couldn't be angry at James because she knew this was true. But she stared at him as if to say, "I'm frustrated, and I don't want to admit you're right."

Tight-lipped, James left the room to go back and finish some inventory work in the freezer.

Emma watched James leave. Gretchen watched Emma watch James.

Gretchen: I see you.

Emma, *embarrassed*: What?

Gretchen: Don't worry. Your secret's safe with me. "We don't talk about people who aren't here," *she said in her best James voice.*

They both laughed. The girls smiled at each other as though they were now secret sisters.

Emma: Is it that obvious?

Gretchen: To me it is. Don't worry, he doesn't have a clue.

Emma, *with a fallen face*: You don't think he likes me?

Gretchen: Oh, I didn't say that. I definitely did not say that!

Emma's eyes and smile both widened.

Chapter 24

A few days later

James and Ron were power washing the siding on Ron's house.

Ron: James, when we're done, let's go do your house and surprise your mom.

James: Okay.

Ron: Then we can go do everyone else's house on the block?

James: Sounds good.

Ron: And the rest of the city.

James: Uh huh.

Ron: James!

James, *snapping out of a daydream*: What? Oh, sorry. What did you say?

Ron: All right James. Spill it. What are you thinking about way far away?

James, *hesitating, because he didn't want to let Ron in, but he respected and needed Ron's advice*: Umm … okay … well … umm …, there's this girl at Roma's.

Ron, *smiling*: Yeah? And you like her?

James, *sheepishly*: Yeah.

Ron: Does she like you?

James: I don't know. I kind of think so. She's starting to give me a hard time.

Ron, *snickering*: Neil constantly gives you a hard time. Does that mean *he* likes you?

James, *laughing*: You know what I mean. She kind of flirts that way.

Ron: I see. Does she "flirt" with the other boys?

James: No. She's nice to them.

Ron: So, she's really nice to them, but she *doesn't* like them. But you she gives a hard time to, and that makes you think she's flirting.

James: Yes.

Ron, *teasingly sarcastic*: Sounds like true love. What's your plan?

James: Plan?

Ron: Yes. What are you going to do about this girl that you think about instead of your work?

James: I guess I'll ask her out.

Ron: After you ask her father's permission.

James: What?! No way!

Ron: Why not?

James: Nobody does that?

Ron: You aren't nobody. Do you seriously like this girl?

James: Yes.

Ron: Then you need to ask her father's permission.

James: Why?

Ron: I have a daughter. I care about her. I have worked hard to build a relationship with her and lead her well so that she won't want to marry any old punk that comes along. I set a high standard for how she should be treated by men so that she would have a high standard for herself. When a boy wanted to date her, she told him he had to come see me first.

James: Did any come see you?

Ron: Not many, but a few did.

James: Did they pass the test?

Ron: I liked some better than others. But right away, the fact that they came to see me started them off on the right foot. Later, my daughter would ask my opinion, and I'd give it to her.

James: Did she listen?

Ron: She did.

James: Oh man!

James looked lost in thought. Finally, he asked.

James: Okay, Mr. Powers. What do I say?

Chapter 25

The next day, in the Roma's parking lot

James was anxious. His nerve came and went as he watched for the black SUV. It looked like a mafia hitman car. James had not been able to see Emma's father through the tinted windows. His imagination was getting the best of him.

Finally, the truck pulled into the parking lot and rolled up to the door. James sprang from near the building and ran out to meet the truck just as Emma had shut the door. James hurried up to the driver's side window. It lowered. A sophisticated, but friendly looking woman was sitting in the driver's seat, looking pleasantly at James.

James: Uh … I … is … are you Emma's mom?

Mrs. Johnson: Yes.

James: Is … okay … um … Is your husband going to be picking her up tonight?

Mom: No, my husband has a meeting tonight. Do you need to speak to him?

"She knows," thought James!

James: Yes!

James froze. After a painfully long ten seconds, Emma's mom rescued him and broke the silence.

Mom: Why don't you come by our house. Tomorrow is Saturday, and my husband should be up and going any time after 8. He has somewhere to be at 11:00 a.m.

James: Okay, I'll be there. What's your address?

She wrote it down and handed it to him.

Mom, *with a twinkle in her eye*: I can see why she's been talking about you.

James: What?

Mom: Goodbye, James.

She drove off.

Chapter 26

As James walked back to the restaurant door, he was full of excitement. *"She's been talking about me?"* He was also full of fear. *"What will her father be like?"* His imagination was running wild with what might happen Saturday morning. In his nervousness, he thought, *"I can't wait to get this over with."*

He was looking forward to spending the shift with Emma, but as he came up to the door, he sensed something was wrong. He could see all the customers were frozen in place. What was going on? He opened the door and knew immediately that Neil was in a rage. He was yelling at someone in the back, but the sound was carrying into the dining area. James hurried back to shush Neil because it was disturbing the customers.

Neil, *screaming*: You called my uncle, didn't you?

Emma: No, I didn't.

Neil: Then, why did he call me last night?

Emma: I don't know.

Neil: He never asks as many questions as he did last night.

Emma, *intimidated, but calmly connecting some dots*: Neil, your uncle is friends with my dad. That's how I found out about this job.

Neil: So what?

Emma: And my dad asks me how things are going.

Just then James turned a corner into the back of the kitchen where they were standing. He saw Emma cornered with Neil's finger pointed at her face.

James, *whispering and motioning with his hands*: Shhh. All the customers can hear you.

Neil, *at the same volume*: I don't care who can hear me.

James, *a little louder, but still subdued*: Neil, you're going to get us all in trouble.

Neil: Oh, you're in trouble all right. My uncle thinks I'm not doing a good job. And I know who probably told him—one of you two.

Emma: I haven't said anything to him.

Neil, *pointing at Emma again*: Then your old man probably did.

James pushed Neil's hand down.

James: Calm down, man, … and stop pointing at Emma.

Neil, *screaming even louder:* Don't tell *me* what to do. *I'm* the puppet master, and *you* are all my puppets! *I* pull the strings around here, and don't forget it.

At first James was stunned. He couldn't believe what Neil just said. He knew Neil viewed everyone on the team as below him, but to actually admit it, and loud enough for the customers to hear?! James had put up with Neil's criticism. He had stood up for Neil when the others talked badly about him. He had done a lot of Neil's work to keep things going. But this was too far. Everyone had put up with quite enough from this jerk. It would feel so good to teach him a lesson. He started pulling back his fist to punch Neil in the face. But someone nearby cleared his throat very loudly.

They all looked around some equipment to see … Mr. Wallace.

Neil panicked. He hurriedly walked past the man, through the dining room, and right out the door.

Mr. Wallace: Hello, Emma and James.

Emma: Hello, Mr. Wallace.

James looked back and forth between them, but he didn't know what to say. He was in shock.

Mr. Wallace, *with a pained look on his face*: I'd like to have a word with James here.

Emma: Certainly. She left the kitchen promptly.

Mr. Wallace: James, would you wait here a moment? I'll be right back.

James: Yes, sir.

Mr. Wallace went to the dining room and apologized to everyone for the outburst in the kitchen. He notified them that they would not be receiving a bill after they had eaten. They went from dead silent to buzzing with discussion and laughter.

Then Mr. Wallace turned to walk back to James in the kitchen. James didn't know what to do. Should he run out the door like Neil had. Maybe Neil wasn't so dumb after all. Would he be fired?

Mr. Wallace: James, you realize Neil is my nephew?

James, *with obvious fear in his eyes*: Yes, sir.

Mr. Wallace: And you realize this is my restaurant.

James: Yes, sir.

Mr. Wallace: And what kind of atmosphere do you think I'm trying to create here?

James: Well, according to Paul, you want a place where people can come and enjoy themselves and relax.

Mr. Wallace: Paul?

James: The previous manager.

Mr. Wallace: Yes, I remember. And would you say that's what it was like when Paul was here?

James: Definitely.

Mr. Wallace: And is that what it has been like since Paul left?

James: Well … uh … hmm.

Mr. Wallace: You can be honest.

James: No, sir.

Mr. Wallace: Hmm. Well, I should have listened to Paul.

James: Sir?

Mr. Wallace: Paul suggested you should be the new manager, but I was concerned you might be too young, and my brother insisted his son could take the job instead. Neil hasn't had much luck with his last few jobs, and my brother thought he needed a better atmosphere.

James: Oh.

Mr. Wallace: I think he needs more than atmosphere. *He paused.* Maybe he needs what you were about to give him.

James, *embarrassed that Mr. Wallace had seen him, then realizing Mr. Wallace was approving. He couldn't contain his smile*: Maybe so.

Mr. Wallace: James, I'm wondering if you would like to manage this place.

James: Are you serious?

Mr. Wallace: Very.

James: I'm not in trouble?

Mr. Wallace: On the contrary. After Emma's dad tipped me off to how things were going around here, I've been talking to some of your co-workers ..., and Neil. It sounds like you've been managing this place for some time now.

James, *humbly*: In some ways, I guess.

Mr. Wallace: So, I was wondering if you would accept a promotion and a raise to make it official?

James: YES, SIR!

Mr. Wallace: And the raise should probably be retroactive to cover the work you have been doing.

James: Thank you.

Mr. Wallace: We should notify some people about this change. Would you come with me?

James wasn't sure what he meant by that. They walked up to the dining room and stood still. Mr. Wallace looked ready to make another announcement. A hush fell on the room. James recognized most of these customers, as they were regulars.

Mr. Wallace, *motioning toward James*: Folks, I would like to introduce you to our new manager!

The room burst into clapping and cheers. The loudest applause came from James's co-workers. He had never experienced anything like this before. It was like a dream … like he was winning some huge prize. The rest of the shift was full of laughter. It didn't take long for someone to suggest they do Saturday night pizza that night, even though it was Friday. They loved the idea. This was worth celebrating. And while they were eating, each co-worker retold parts of what just happened. James was so encouraged, especially when Emma would smile at him with admiration.

Chapter 27

The next morning all the glory had faded. James was terrified as he stood at the front door of Emma's very nice, and very large house. He couldn't decide if he should knock on the imposing door or ring the doorbell. While he was deliberating, the door opened. A giant of a man managed to make the huge double doors look small. He had a complete lack of expression. James assumed the man knew why he was there, but he was giving James no help whatsoever.

James: Good morning. I … uh … I work at Roma's.

This was *not* what James had rehearsed. He had written down every single word he would say, and he had practiced saying it in every way possible.

"Hello, I'm JAMES, it's nice to MEET you … HELLO, I'm James, it's NICE to meet YOU … Hello, I AM James, IT'S nice to meet you!"

But none of that was coming out now. He just stared, waiting for Emma's dad, Mr. Johnson, to respond.

Mr. Johnson, *after scrutinizing James a long time*: You must be James. Why don't you come in, son?

James followed the giant into the house, which was beautifully decorated with a woman's touch, and into a study that was both a scholarly library and elegant man-cave. There was a whole wall of trophies, photos, and sports memorabilia. James, who was a huge football fan, was drawn to it. As he looked at the shelves and the walls, he noticed several pictures of Mr. Johnson in uniform.

James's heart skipped a beat. This was Clarence Johnson? He was a local football legend in his day who was now a federal judge. Would he know about James's record? James broke into a sweat and his vision blurred. His mind simply could not process the fact that he was here to ask this man for the permission to date his only daughter. His gaze fell to a picture of the giant with his baby girl. He held her and looked into the cameras in a way that said, "If *anyone* even *thinks* about harming my girl ...."

James was rescued from the terror of his imagination by Mr. Johnson's voice.

Mr. Johnson: James, why don't you have a seat?

He pointed to a chair across the desk from his own. James felt like he was back in the courtroom in front of the judge. Then he realized he was.

Mr. Johnson: How can I help you?

That was what he said, but James heard: "*Who do you think you are? I hope you are not here to do what I think you are here to do. Go ahead, make my day.*"

James thought of Ron's stare and tried it out. He broke it in half a second and looked at the floor.

"Come on, James," he told himself. "Look him in the eye. He can't kill you here." He took a deep breath and forced his eyes onto the man.

James: I would like your permission to ask Emma out on a date.

There was an interminably long silence. Mr. Johnson looked at him first with a frown, which changed to inquisitiveness, which, after a painfully long time, gave way to a smile. This was good. James started to hope.

Mr. Johnson: No.

James was stunned.

James: Okay. Well, thank you for your time.

Mr. Johnson: I appreciate you asking me, son. I admire that. But the fact is, we've told Emma that she cannot date until she is seventeen. That's almost a year away. On-top-of-that, I don't know you. I don't know your parents.

James was at first relieved to think Mr. Johnson did not know much about him, then realized that by mentioning this, it was likely he would eventually want to know much more about James than whatever news Emma brought home from Roma's.

Mr. Johnson: This is my only daughter. My little girl. She is precious to me. It concerns me very much who she spends time with. Thanks for coming by James. It was a manly thing to do. I do genuinely appreciate it.

James: Yes, sir. Thanks for your time.

The big man stood up, and James followed his lead. They walked back through the house. James was crestfallen. Then he was angry. How could this man just shut him down like this? Maybe James would just try to see her behind her parents' backs. But he thought about Paul and Ron and realized quickly that he needed to accept the man's decision. He would not pursue dating Emma yet, even though most boys would. If he did that, then this was only for show. No, he would respect her father's wishes.

They got to the door, and Mr. Johnson opened it for James, who walked through it, shaking hands firmly with the man. He walked out and got as far as the steps.

Mr. Johnson: James.

He stopped and turned.

Mr. Johnson: I like you, and I appreciate what you've done here—that you were brave enough to come here in person and speak with me, and you didn't argue with my decision. If you were the kind of person who would go behind my back and try to date my daughter anyway, I would be able to tell right away. I didn't get to be a federal judge by not being able to read people.

You can't take her out on a date, but why don't you come back tomorrow at 5:30? You can eat dinner with us, and then maybe you and Emma can hang out together in the family room afterward.

James was stunned … and elated.

James: Okay! Yes, sir, I'll be back then.

Mr. Johnson: And I want to thank you. I heard that you stood up for Emma when she was having trouble with Neil.

James nodded.

Mr. Johnson: And I heard you just earned a promotion.

James was speechless. He would have smiled if he wasn't so scared.

Mr. Johnson: See you tomorrow, son.

James: Yeah …yes, sir. Okay. Thanks. Thank you.

James didn't remember his feet touching the ground on the way home.

Chapter 28

The next night James showed up promptly with some flowers that Jackie helped him pick from her garden. *"Make sure they know these are for Mrs. Johnson,"* she had said.

Mrs. Johnson: Thank you so much, James. I'll put these in some water. They'll go nicely on the table.

Emma, *bashfully*: Hi, James. You made it past Papa Pit Bull.

James laughed. The two went into the kitchen. Mr. Johnson was helping his wife finish getting things ready. He was plating the kabobs he had just brought in from the grill on the back porch.

Mr. Johnson: I hope you like steak.

James: It's my favorite.

Mr. Johnson: We used to have pizza on Sunday nights, but for some reason Emma has been getting tired of pizza.

James laughed.

Mrs. Johnson: Emma, see what James wants to drink.

James: Water is fine.

Emma: Are you sure? We have Dr. Pepper, Coke, and tea. Also, milk.

James: Coke.

Mr. Johnson, *bringing the platter of kabobs and grilled vegetables to the center of the table*: Voila!

Mrs. Johnson brought a huge loaf of bread from the oven and set it down. Everything smelled great!

Mr. Johnson: James, why don't you sit here?

James obeyed and took the seat across from Emma. He started to sit down, but then realized the family was still standing. Once Mrs. Johnson sat down, Emma sat down, and then Mr. Johnson. James followed suit. Mrs. Johnson began to pile food onto his plate. James looked at it gratefully.

Mrs. Johnson: Emma told us what happened at Roma's Friday night. Sounds like it was about time for that.

James blushed and didn't know what to say, although he felt very pleased.

Emma: He's going to do a great job.

As the night went on, James was feeling more and more comfortable with the Johnsons. Once dinner was over, he offered to help clean up. Mrs. Johnson shooed him away saying something about James being their guest, and why doesn't Emma show him the game room downstairs. Maybe they could watch a movie. Mr. Johnson was quick to point out that there were security cameras down there. James did not know if he was kidding, but he determined to take the threat seriously.

Chapter 29

Downstairs

Emma: My dad likes you.

James: He said that?

Emma: No, but I can tell. My mom does, too.

James: I asked him if I could ask you on a date. He said no.

Emma: My parents have always said I can date once I'm seventeen.

James: Why so old?

Emma: They don't want me to get hurt playing games.

James: Oh.

Emma: And they believe dating is about getting to know someone I might marry someday. So, they don't want me dating until I'm ready to think about getting married.

James flushed at this, and his heart skipped a beat.

Emma: But I do think that they might make an exception for the spring formal at my school if they come as chaperones.

James: Why do you say that?

Emma: My mom's been asking questions about it.

James's wheels were turning. The spring formal wasn't for another two months, but he would need to save up for it. It was an expensive deal, and he had had no intention of going before now, as such things were a waste of time and money. Funny how his mind had changed. He'd sell his left arm to come up with the money now.

The rest of the night went wonderfully. The two talked for a couple of hours, and then Mr. Johnson came down at ten and said it was time for James to go home. He offered him a ride, but James said he would like to walk. He needed to process all of this. Emma walked him outside.

Emma: Thanks for coming to talk to my dad. It impressed him.

James: Just *him*?

Emma: *And* my mom.

James was waiting for more.

Emma, *her face blooming into a beautiful smile*: And me.

With that, she turned to go back inside.

James floated home again. He didn't even remember the walk, just that he found himself in the living room of his house with his mother was asking, "How did it go?"

James: Good.

Olivia: Good?

James, *grinning ear to ear*: REAL GOOD!

He went into his room to count his "spend" money before going to bed.

Chapter 30

The next week James and Ron were digging up some overgrown bushes from the garden to make more room for vegetables. They were talking as they worked.

James: I looked it up. $150 for a tuxedo, $100 for dinner. $80 for two tickets.

Ron, *whistling*: Things sure have changed since I was in school. Do you have $330?

James: In my "save" money.

Ron: Hmm.

James: What?

Ron: Huh?

James: What? You said, "Hmm." You never "Hmm" for no reason. What are you thinking?

Ron: Well … you are doing such a great job with your money and work, and I'm really proud of you, but you might consider one thing.

James: What is it?

Ron: It's your "save" money. I think you ought to at least consider the idea that "save" means a little longer term than you're thinking.

James: What? But I saved it. What am I saving it for?

Ron: Something bigger and further down the road. If I were your age, I know exactly what I would do.

James, *knowing he is beaten already*: And what is that?

Ron: Well, if you were to start thinking of that money as untouchable right now, you would be able invest it soon, and then your money would start working for you.

James: What do you mean?

Ron: If you invest your money it grows over time. That way, while you are working to make money, some of your money is also working to make money for you. Eventually, if you get enough money working for you, your money will make more money than you do.

Ron tried to explain how compounding works, but it wasn't making much sense to James. Ron went into the house to pull out a chart from his briefcase. Upon returning, he showed James that if he saved $300 per month for forty years, growing at 8 percent, James would have over a million dollars. He pointed to various amounts and time frames for James until he had grasped the implications of his current age and earning potential. James started to get excited about the possibilities.

Ron: A word of caution—I'm not saying be a miser. Budget and spend your "spend" money. Enjoy it. Be generous with your "give" money. But with your "save" money, determine to wait a long time before even considering spending that. Even then, only spend what you're making on it, leave the principal alone.

James: What is principal?

Ron: That is the total amount that you put in to do all the work for you. Someday, if you do it right, you'll be able to live on the interest, the money that the principal is earning for you.

James: And then I can take it easy and do nothing for the rest of my life!

Ron: Not so fast! Work is a privilege and a way to contribute to society. I never intend to stop working in one way or another, but what you will have is the freedom to do whatever kind of work you want, even if you don't get paid.

James: Why would I work for nothing?

Ron: Do you remember how you felt when you helped Gretchen's mother?

James: Yeah, it felt pretty good.

Ron: Well volunteering is a way to do that over and over. Work isn't primarily about earning money.

James: What is it about then? I can't think of any other reason to make pizzas. It's not my dream job!

Ron, *laughing*: I understand. You're a teenager working your first job, but it's only the beginning. It will lead you to the next thing, and then the next thing until you are working in a field that you love, if you do it right.

James, *smiling*: Mom showed me your pyramid scheme.

Ron, *humored*: Good. But even while you're working a not-so-fun job, just the simple act of working is of great value.

James: I remember you talking like this when I first started working with you at your house. It was hard to understand then, but I really think I get it now. I honestly don't feel any passion for making pizza, but I get a good feeling after we handle a lunch rush and have the place ready for the dinner crowd. I love it when I get faster or figure a way to do something better than before.

Ron: That's it, James. Think like that, and the money will follow. All that's left is to handle it well.

James: Right. So, money for the spring formal. What do you think I should do?

Ron: What do *you* think you should do?

James: *Save* up my *spend* money?

Ron: Bingo! That's what I would do.

James: Well, that settles it!

Both laughed as James good-naturedly continued to give his mentor a hard time.

James went home that night and made a budget that included saving 90 percent of his "spend" money for the formal. This would make everything tight until afterward, but Emma wasn't allowed to date and going to hang out with her family was free! James made a list of other ways he could spend his time and be entertained for free since this was going to be his only option for the next month.

Chapter 31

A year later

Mr. Wallace: James, you have done a fine job managing this restaurant.

James's face brightened up. The last time Mr. Wallace said this, James received a raise.

James: Thank you, sir.

Mr. Wallace: But I'm not planning to give you a raise.

James, *trying to hide his disappointment*: Oh.

Mr. Wallace: I want to give you an opportunity, instead.

James, *curiously*: Okay.

Mr. Wallace: I have three different restaurants. This one was my first, I have such great memories building this business. But it's also the farthest from where I live. What would you think of buying this restaurant and becoming the new owner?

James, *in shock*: I … the thought never crossed my mind.

Mr. Wallace: You've chosen not to go to college.

James, *awkwardly defensive*: Well … I don't know…

Mr. Wallace interrupted him.

Mr. Wallace: I'm not saying there's anything wrong with that. I never went to college.

James relaxed.

Mr. Wallace: James, you are good with people, you are good with your hands, and you are good with money. You have a natural business sense.

James, *obviously pleased*: Thank you.

Mr. Wallace: This was my first business. Why would I sell it to you?

James: I was wondering the same thing?

Mr. Wallace: I won't be here someday, but I would feel good about someone running this store who is taking good care of our customers. I think you are the person to do that.

James: I don't know what to say.

Mr. Wallace: You don't need to say or decide anything. You can't buy the business until you are eighteen, which I believe is still several months away. In the meantime, I'll get together some numbers to go over with you. You will need to know the whole financial picture so you can make an informed decision. Then, if you decide to move ahead, I'll start showing you how to do the books, and who I contact for maintenance issues—things like that.

James: Thank you, sir. I appreciate your offer.

James was grateful to Mr. Wallace, but he also felt good about himself and the direction of his life.

Epilogue

A few days after Mr. Wallace offered the restaurant to James, there was a knock at Ron and Jackie's door.

Ron expected to see James, but it was Olivia.

Ron, *opening the door*: Hi, Olivia. How are you doing?

Olivia: Hi, Ron. Hi, Jackie. I think James told you about the offer Mr. Wallace made.

Jackie: To buy the restaurant? Yes. James was beaming with pride when he told us.

Ron: We are so proud of him, and you.

Olivia: I don't know how to thank you, Ron, for all the time you've spent with James, and all the lessons you've taught him.

Ron: There's no need to.

Olivia, *interrupting*: Not only that but helping me with my own job situation.

Ron: Really, there's no need to.

Olivia, *interrupting again*: I asked Jackie if you had a favorite dessert and she said you might be interested in some chocolate chip cookies.

She pulled a platter of cookies from behind her back.

Ron: Well, in that case, go ahead and thank me!

They all laughed. Then Jackie offered Olivia a cup of coffee and they sampled the cookies together.

Olivia: I've been having Michael do chores around the house. He didn't like the idea at first, but he's getting used to it now.

Jackie and Ron, *in unison*: Good for you.

Olivia: I think Michael is going to follow my footsteps and go to college. He's really applying himself at school.

Jackie: Aren't you proud of him?

Olivia: You know it. But I might need to ask your advice about next steps?

Ron: I'm at your service, especially if you are paying me with cookies.

They all laughed again.

ꕤ ꕤ

James and Emma attended the spring formal and dated for another two and a half years, initially at her parent's house. As Mr. Wallace handed more responsibility to James, he spent less time with Ron Powers, but he still found time to visit the Johnson family on a regular basis. He spent most of his time with Emma, but he also spent a lot of time with Mr. Johnson. He taught James many things about being an honorable and responsible man—things like keeping his word and being able to say "yes" and "no" to himself. He also taught him practical things about everything from legal matters to insurance to investing to home repairs.

ꟈ ꟈ

When he turned 18, James bought Roma's from Mr. Wallace. There were many pleasant surprises and big disappointments, but over time, he developed a team of young people who enjoyed working together, and the restaurant ran smoothly. This team often talked about how they could make things even better, and the customers seemed to appreciate most of the changes they tried. The place kept getting busier.

Mr. Wallace would stop in from time to time to watch what was happening—with great satisfaction. He eventually approached James about buying out his other restaurants, one at a time. James felt overwhelmed each time, but Mr. Wallace gave him a strategy for training and promoting key leaders to run each location. He also offered to finance the restaurants over time. It was a win-win situation for them both as Mr. Wallace would receive passive income for many years from selling the restaurants, including the interest payments on these private loans. James would be able to buy them without going through the bank for lending.

Eventually, James worked up the nerve to ask Mr. and Mrs. Johnson if he could marry Emma. They had always pictured her marrying someone with a college education, but it was clear James was going to be a successful businessman and would be able to take good care of their daughter. It was also clear that James and Emma loved each other very much. They gave the couple their blessing.

APPENDIX I

Discussion Questions about the Benefits of Work

Feel satisfaction

- Do you ever remember feeling a sense of satisfaction from your work?
- Why do you think that happens?
- How does work build self-esteem?

Learn independence

- Why is it important to learn to pay your own expenses?
- How does making your own decisions instill a sense of responsibility and confidence?

Spend money

- Why do you think it is so enjoyable to buy what you need and want with money you have earned?

Meet friends

- Describe the feeling of being part of a team. If you have not experienced this, what do you imagine it would feel like?

Give to those in need

- Why do you think it is so personally encouraging to help other people?

Save money

- What does delayed gratification mean?
- How does learning to manage money lead to delayed gratification and preparation for future needs and dreams?

Learn

- What benefit of work do you value the most—the opportunity to gain social skills, acquire technical information, or develop vocational skills?

Succeed

- ❖ How does being faithful with small opportunities sometimes leads to bigger opportunities?
- ❖ Is it more important to you to climb the corporate ladder or to find work you love?

Stay healthy

- ❖ How does work contribute to physical and mental health?

APPENDIX II

Maybe it's not the right time or place for your child to have a formal job, but they want to generate some extra money. Here is a brainstormed list of ideas to discuss. The possibilities are endless.

LAWN/HOME CARE:

Mowing lawns

Raking leaves

Shoveling snow

Sealing driveways

Painting addresses on curbs

Cleaning windows

Stocking softener salt

Cleaning or replacing furnace filters

House cleaning

Pool service (sweeping, testing, adding chemicals, etc.)

Cleaning out basements, attics, yards, garages

Hosting garage sales

House-sitting

Removing old Christmas trees

Painting

SELLING:

Homemade baked goods

Candy or beverages at public venues or events

Buying and reselling jeans or sneakers

American flags

Holiday gifts or treats

Firewood

Collecting returnable cans or other recyclable materials and turning them in for money

T-shirts

Golf balls

House plants

Homemade greeting cards

Fruits or vegetables

SERVICE WORK:

Valet parking

Waiting on tables at a restaurant … then a nicer one … then a nicer one

Babysitting or childcare

Pet sitting/dog walking

Stocking bird feeders

Photography

Graphic arts

Setting up websites for others

Setting up or repairing computers

Gift wrapping

Tutoring

Generation Series

Experience the whole Generation Series through four business parables, encountering interesting characters who reveal practical insights about work, money, and living to the fullest. But be careful, the trajectory of your life might change in the process.

Book 1 – **Kids Work**

The Benefits They Receive When Kids Work. Meet James, who starts out torn between a gang and the law and his neighbor, Ron Powers. Will he go to the juvenile center? Will he work with Ron? How will his decisions affect the direction of his life? This fast-moving business parable illustrates how enabling kids to work brings many benefits and prepares them for the real world, including ways you may have never considered.

Book 2 – **Dream House**

Dream House Debt Free 8-12 Years From Now. Eavesdrop as Ron Powers teaches his niece, Sophie, how she can acquire her dream house, and pay it off in 8-12 years. They bond over time, and she applies many of his practical tips to improve her personal cash flow. Includes ideas you can use too.

Book 3 – **Retire Successfully**

Seven Key Areas Needed to Retire Successfully. We met Sophie in Dream House. One of her workmates asks her how to prepare for a great retirement and she is happy to share her secrets. Follow her example and you could be ready for your own successful retirement adventure.

Book 4 – **Legacy Living**

Be Rich Through Legacy Living. After Lydia is very disturbed by a dream, her cousin, Jackie Powers, introduces her to some unforgettable people. She will never be the same … and you might not either.

Would you like to connect with the author? Please feel free to reach out: **craig@famfocfinancial.com**.

FAMILY FOCUSED
FINANCIAL

Family Focused Financial specializes in retirement planning and services. Securities and Advisory Services are offered through ***Harbour Investments, Inc.***

Contact:
Phone: 269-208-4237
Email: Info@famfocfinancial.com
Website: www.famfocfinancial.com

Made in the USA
Monee, IL
04 November 2026

67379950R00069